I0817228

EARTH
Renae Gilles and
Warren Rylands
EYEDISCOVER

Go to www.eyediscover.com and enter this book's unique code.

BOOK CODE

AVS48897

EYEDISCOVER brings you optic readalongs that support active learning.

Published by AV² by Weigl
350 5th Avenue, 59th Floor New York, NY 10118
Website: www.eyediscover.com

Library of Congress Control Number: 2018951106

ISBN 978-1-4896-8007-5 (hardcover)

Printed in the United States of America
in Brainerd, Minnesota
1 2 3 4 5 6 7 8 9 0 22 21 20 19 18

082018
120917

Project Coordinator: John Willis
Designer: Mandy Christiansen

Weigl acknowledges Alamy, Getty Images, and Shutterstock as the primary image suppliers for this title.

EYEDISCOVER provides enriched content, optimized for tablet use, that supplements and complements this book. EYEDISCOVER books strive to create inspired learning and engage young minds in a total learning experience.

Watch
Video content brings each page to life.

Browse
Thumbnails make navigation simple.

Read
Follow along with text on the screen.

Listen
Hear each page read aloud.

Your EYEDISCOVER Optic Readalongs come alive with...

Audio
Listen to the entire book read aloud.

Video
High resolution videos turn each spread into an optic readalong.

OPTIMIZED FOR

- TABLETS
- WHITEBOARDS
- COMPUTERS
- AND MUCH MORE!

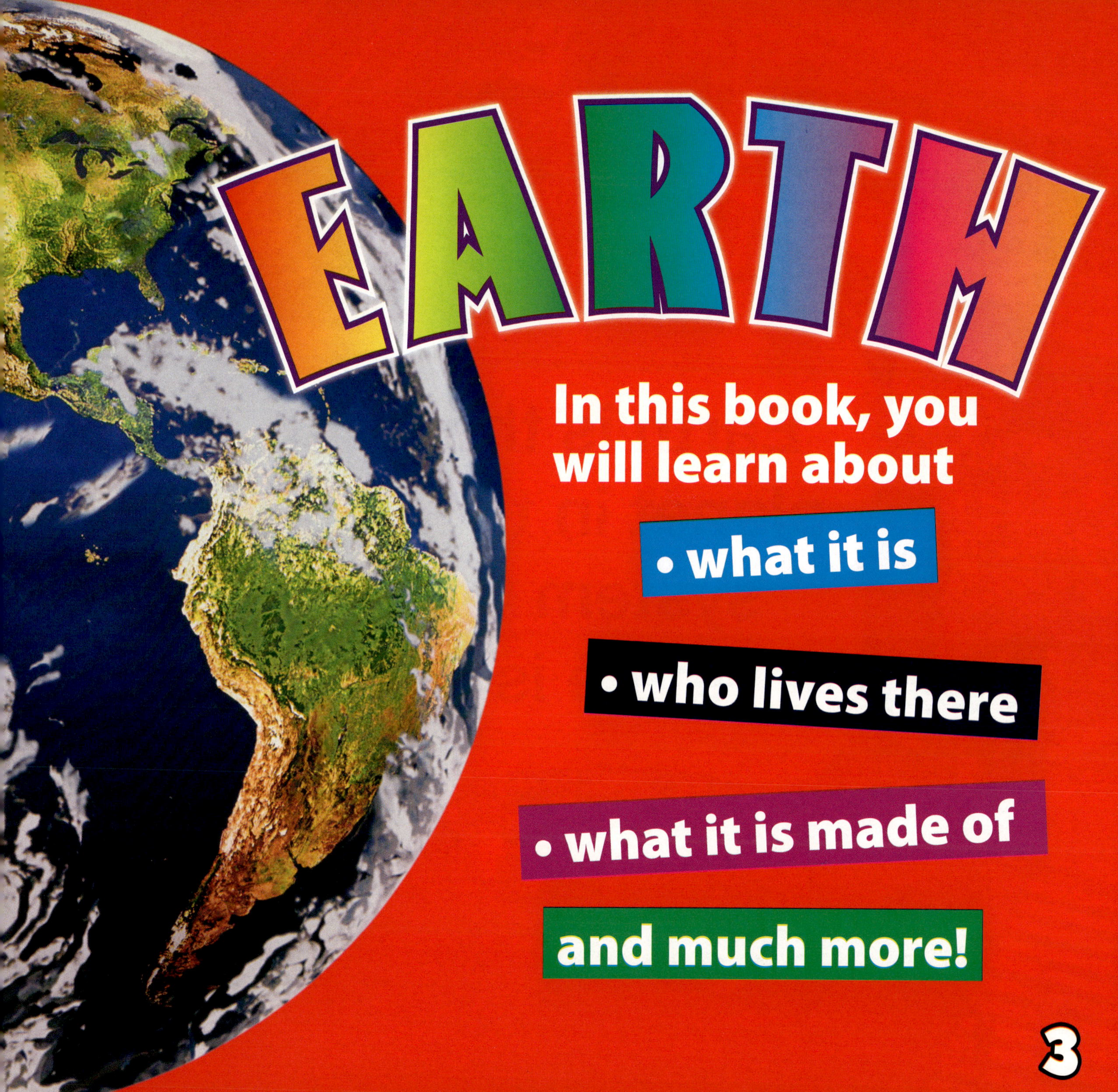
EARTH
In this book, you will learn about
• what it is
• who lives there
• what it is made of
and much more!

Earth is the only planet in the solar system where there is life.

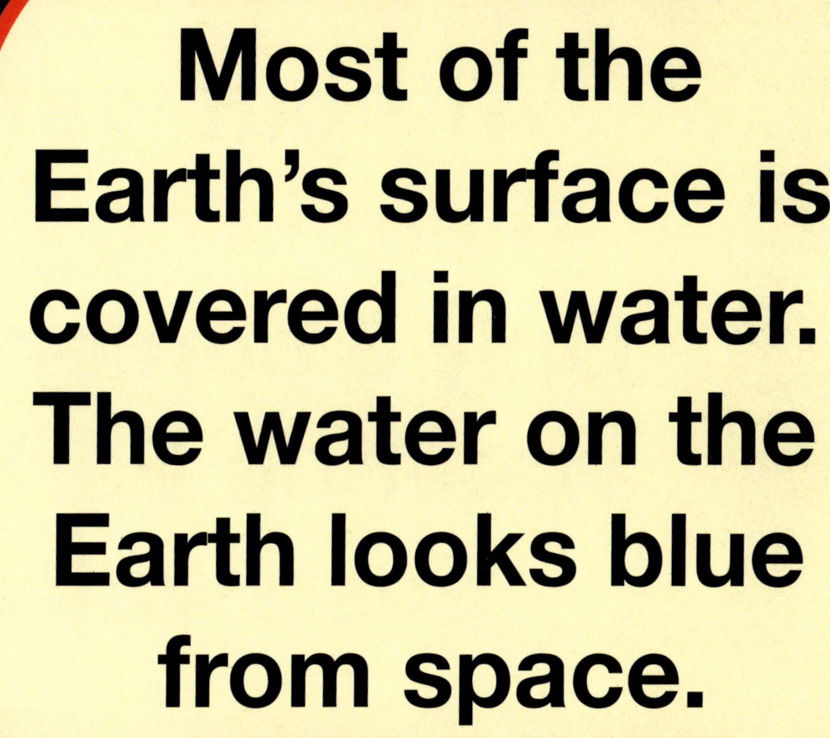

Most of the Earth's surface is covered in water. The water on the Earth looks blue from space.

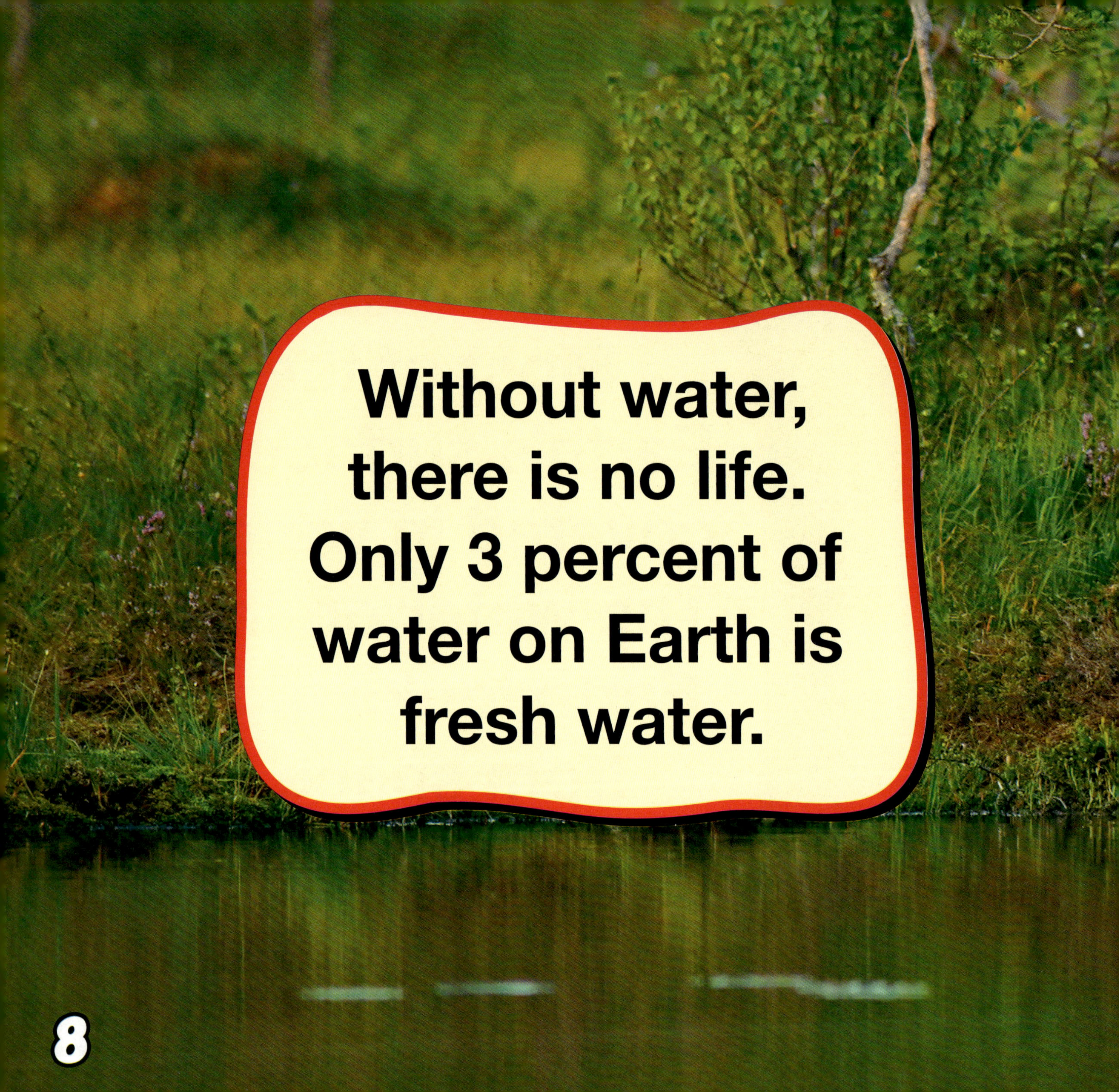

Without water, there is no life. Only 3 percent of water on Earth is fresh water.

The rest of Earth's water is salt water. Most of it is found in Earth's oceans. The oceans are home to more than 1 million animals.

Trees are very important to life on Earth. Without trees, there would not be enough fresh air.

Trees also give us food. There are about 3,000 different types of fruit found in the Earth's rainforests.

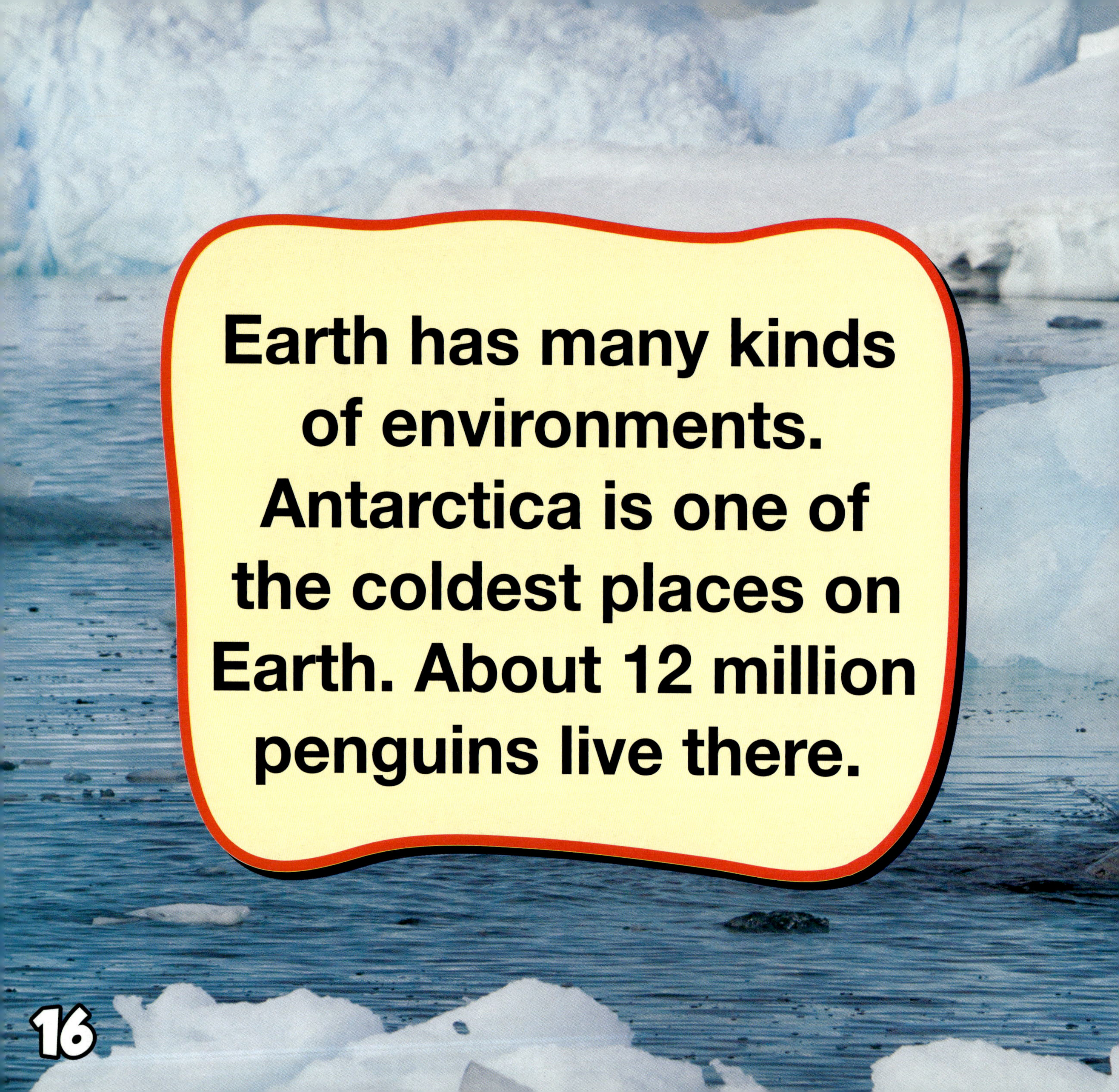

Earth has many kinds of environments. Antarctica is one of the coldest places on Earth. About 12 million penguins live there.

The Sahara Desert is one of the hottest and driest places on Earth. Many insects, like dung beetles, live there.

Keeping the Earth healthy is very important. All living things on Earth need clean air and water.

There are between **12,000** and **15,000** different kinds of **butterflies** in the world.

Lake Superior, along the United States-Canada border, is the **largest lake** in the **world**.

Lightning
strikes Earth about
8.6 million
times per day.

Earth has
one moon.
The moon travels
around the Earth.

There are
7.6 billion
people on **Earth.**

KEY WORDS

Research has shown that as much as 65 percent of all written material published in English is made up of 300 words. These 300 words cannot be taught using pictures or learned by sounding them out. They must be recognized by sight. This book contains 49 common sight words to help young readers improve their reading fluency and comprehension. This book also teaches young readers several important content words, such as proper nouns. These words are paired with pictures to aid in learning and improve understanding.

Page	Sight Words First Appearance
4	Earth, in, is, life, only, the, there, where
7	from, looks, most, of, on, water
8	no, without
11	animals, are, found, home, it, more, than, to
12	air, be, enough, important, not, trees, very, would
15	about, also, different, food, give, us
16	has, kinds, live, many, one, places
19	and, like
20	all, need, things

Page	Content Words First Appearance
4	planet, solar system
7	space, surface
8	percent
11	million, oceans, salt
15	fruit, rainforests
16	Antarctica, environments, penguins
19	dung beetles, insects, Sahara Desert

Watch
Video content brings each page to life.

Browse
Thumbnails make navigation simple.

Read
Follow along with text on the screen.

Listen
Hear each page read aloud.

Go to www.eyediscover.com and enter this book's unique code.

BOOK CODE

AVS48897